I0766340

DANCES *of* ITALY

BIANCA M. GALANTI

NOVERRE PRESS

TRANSLATED BY
EVELYN S. SPEAR
ILLUSTRATED BY
G. DOUGLAS HALLIDAY
ASSISTANT EDITOR
YVONNE MOYSE

First published in 1953
This edition published in 2021 by
The Noverre Press
Southwold House
Isington Road
Binsted
Hampshire
GU34 4PH

ISBN 978-1-914311-1-26-0

CONTENTS

Illustrations in Colour, pages 2, 12, 29, 39
Map of Italy, page 6

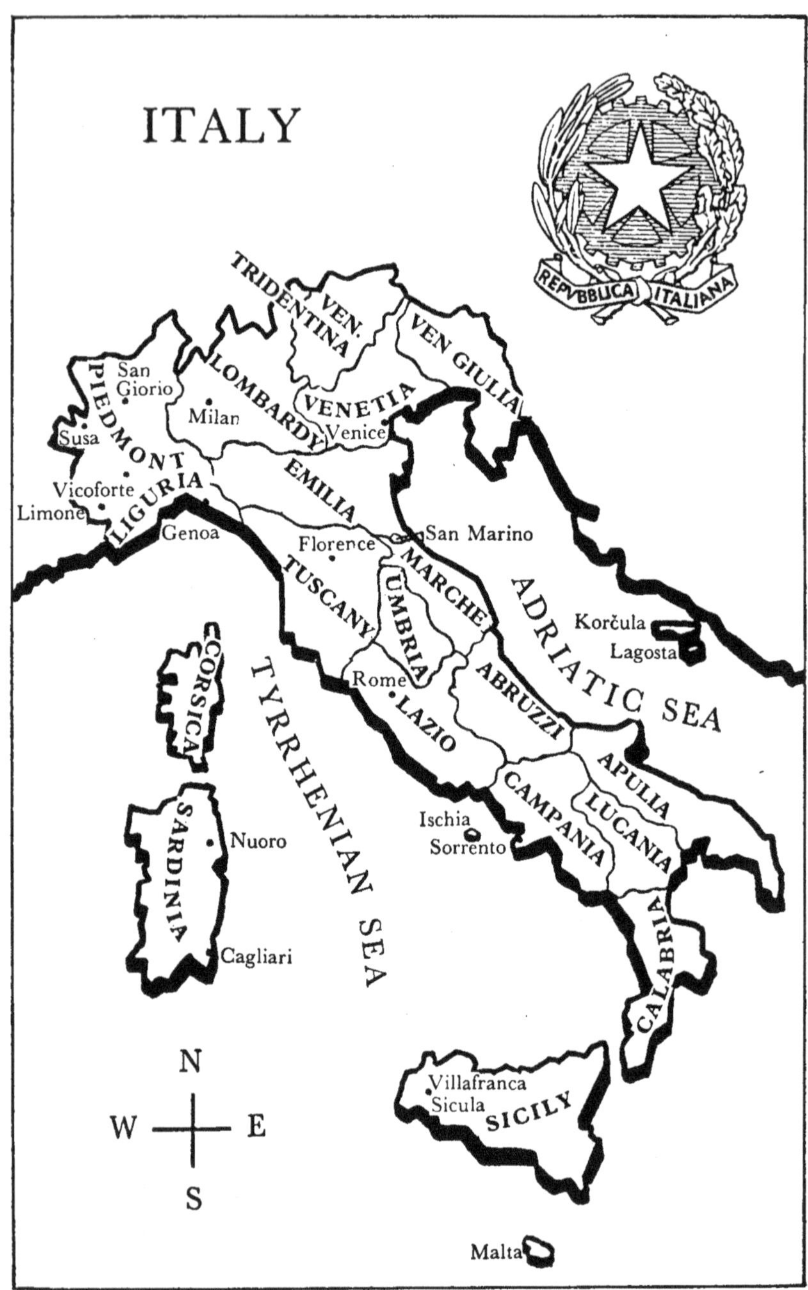

ITALY
REPVBBLICA ITALIANA
TRIDENTINA
VEN. TENTINA
VEN GIULIA
PIEDMONT
San Giorio
LOMBARDY
Milan
VENETIA
Venice
Susa
EMILIA
Vicoforte
LIGURIA
Limone
Genoa
Florence
San Marino
TUSCANY
MARCHE
UMBRIA
ADRIATIC SEA
Korčula
Lagosta
CORSICA
Rome
LAZIO
ABRUZZI
APULIA
TYRRHENIAN SEA
SARDINIA
Nuoro
Ischia
Sorrento
CAMPANIA
LUCANIA
Cagliari
CALABRIA
N
W E
S
Villafranca
Sicula
SICILY
Malta

ALTHOUGH our country has never produced a truly national dance, every region is rich in its own examples and there are as many types and as many variations of some of these types as there are regions. Every occasion is an excuse for dancing—agricultural feasts, betrothals, weddings, public festivals and anniversaries both civil and religious. In summer dancing is out of doors, on a threshing floor, in the fields; in winter indoors, in the inn, even in the stables. Most widely diffused is the so-called erotic type, depicting courtship or used as a nuptial dance. Sometimes the choice is the woman's, as in the Mirror dance (dello Specchio), the Sigh (del Sospiro), the Chair (della Seggiola), or the Married Couple's dance (degli Sposi); sometimes it is the man who carries off—even, one may say, abducts—the woman: indeed the original content of the Romagna Stick dance represented a rape, as does the Dance of the Four Corners (dei Quattro Cantoni).

Piedmont offers an immense variety of dances. There we find the armed dances, for example the Swordsmen of San Giorio (province of Turin) and the beflowered Lachera of Rocca Grimalda (province of Alessandria). Sword dances are also connected with religious festivals, such as that of the Spadonari of Limone or that at Giaglione, Val di Susa, on St. Vincent's Day. Piedmont also owns the Bal del Saber at and around Vicoforte. In Piedmont we find a charming Courting dance, the Monferrina, which, originating in the Monferrato district, has travelled all over Lombardy and Friuli and even into Switzerland. Southwards its type reaches Romagna, where it meets other well-known erotic dances, the Furlana in Friuli and Venetia, the Trescone in Emilia and Tuscany, the Saltarello in many regions, to terminate in the Tarentella, of all Courting dances the most animated.

PROCESSIONAL AND RELIGIOUS DANCES

These form a group apart, displaying a definitely religious background and forming part of actual religious ceremonies. In Calabria we find the survival of a dance by flagellants; at Villafranca Sicula, Sicily, on the second Sunday in May we see the well-known Riattate danced during the festival of the Madonna of the Myrtle. As the procession defiles, a joyful, even ecstatic dance is performed by the faithful, frantically waving branches of laurel and myrtle. Again at Casteltermini one of the main features in the festival of the Invention of the Holy Cross is the Taratatà, a Sword dance.

EROTIC DANCES

We look at the Monferrina, that delightful dance for couples now chiefly seen in Piedmont. It is performed by several couples at once, often accompanied by singing, and shows its character in a series of bows, mimed teasings and coaxings. In the first part the couples promenade round the dancing place. As the music changes they take hands but lean back as though for a swing-round, and the tempo quickens as a cross-step with knee-bending is done. Sometimes a circle is formed for this part. Lastly each pair draws together again, as in Part One.

A well-known couple dance is the Furlana, belonging to the north-eastern part of Italy. Two distinct variants are known, the Furlana Ziguzaine in 3/4 time, widely known in Friuli and danced from time immemorial at public festivals, and another in 6/8 time erroneously called Furlana, not much known in the Friuli region and more probably of Venetian origin. A very old dance, known since the Middle Ages, is the Trescone by four couples forming a square. The women step lightly in their places while the men with lively steps pass from one woman to another, vying with each other in self-assurance and bravura. This is a genuine folk dance of the fields, still performed at the time of certain agricultural work such as picking the hemp and the stripping of Indian corn cobs. The work finished, music— amateur or professional—is called for and everyone starts dancing in the open air. The instruments may be the intruding accordion, sometimes a wind instrument, a 'cello, a guitar, more rarely a mandoline. But in Romagna singing without instruments supplies the air, when the dance is known as Trescone of the Mountain. In older days the Trescone was danced by the guests at a wedding. They divided into two groups, one of singers in a ring round another composed of the four dancing couples.

In Tuscany another change occurs. Here it is the Tresconeto, in quick 6/8 time, known in all villages and districts of Lunigiana and seen always on Old Carnival Sunday—today the first Sunday in Lent owing to the change in the calendar. The rhythm quickens throughout to test the endurance of the dancers.

THE SALTARELLO

In Central Italy the most famous Couple dance is the Saltarello; and when the courting mime is beautifully, even passionately, performed, as it can be, this is indeed an erotic dance. It has been immortalised in the engravings of Bartolomeo and Achille Pinelli and described by nearly every traveller of the last century. It is well known in Romagna, in Lazio (Latium) which is supposed to be its place of origin, and has penetrated to the little Republic of San Marino, to the Marche and the Abruzzi, with constant changes, becoming practically a different dance in different places. The Saltarello, as danced in eighteenth-century Rome and as still danced on some of the country estates in the Roman Campagna, is in reality simple, since it has no fixed steps or figures, although a balancé step is much used. But the mime demands good acting in the love scenes both for man and girl, the one pursuing, the other retreating, the one ardently offering, the other, after much play with her apron, at last accepting. A decisive drum beat indicates a leap by both dancers. This is the only obligatory movement and gave its name to this outstanding declaration of love in dance.

In Ciociaria the Saltarello, contrary to its name, is transformed into a *bassa danza* with low steps instead of the prescribed leaps. This Ciociaria Saltarello is seen chiefly in summer and in the open air, after work in the fields. Always in 3/8 or 6/8 here, it is either a Couple dance or for rings of uneven numbers of people who keep together by interlacing their arms over each other's shoulders, their bodies bent slightly forward, their heads almost knocking together in the centre. Nevertheless this bent attitude manages to remain quite dignified and allows the body to sway with the movement of the feet. The feet, bare for the most part, slide softly about on the ground without jumps, and this is what gives it the characteristics of a *bassa danza*. The accordion player all but takes part in the dance himself, going close to the performers, playing with more and more *brio* to excite and encourage them.

Following its geographical dissemination, we find a Saltarella in the Abruzzi as a foundation for figure dances of some antiquity, for instance the Dance of the Standard (dell' Insegna) at Forcella, province of Teramo, and again under the intriguing name The Love Noose (Laccio d'Amore) at Penna Sant' Andrea.

With yet another form of name we see it in the Marche as Lu Sardarellu, with much leaping to accordion and

small drum, the latter beaten by an elderly woman. A
single couple performs its three figures. The musicians love
to get down from their seats, enter the circle of spectators
and press into the dance. In Romagna two or three couples
dance, the men joining their right hands and performing
somewhat intricate steps opposite one another, gradually
working themselves into a circle; the women show their
skill by placing a glass of water on their heads and lightly
stepping without spilling a drop. Like the Jota of Aragon*
this form of Saltarello has an instrumental part (violin)
followed by a sung part (always a male singer) while the
dancers stand still waiting for the violin to take up the air
again. The sung verses, also like the Jota coplas, sparkle
with malicious *double-entendres* causing much delight to the
listeners.

THE TARANTELLA

This ancient dance lives in Campania, Lucania, Calabria,
Apulia (Puglia), Sicily and Sardinia, each region showing
its own characteristics. It is considered by foreigners to be
Italy's national dance and has been mentioned by many
famous travellers and writers: Madame de Staël, Goethe,
Musset, Lamartine, and many others. Composers have fre-
quently used its distinctive rhythm—one has only to recall
Tarantella forms in the works of Chopin, Mendelssohn and
Liszt. Like the Saltarello it is in 3/8 or 6/8 time, and like
the Saltarello is markedly a Courting dance, miming at-
tack and defence, flattery, and a final love conquest. Round
Naples it is gay, in the Falerno and Massico districts some
figures show a certain solemnity. Exiled now from Naples
except in theatrical guise, it is found in Capri and Sorrento
—and in Sorrento two rival groups of Tarantella dancers,
the Tramontano and the Vittoria, strive for supremacy.
In Apulia it becomes the Tarandla, seen at town and

* See *Dances of Spain* (vol. ii) in this series.

Plate 2
Tarantella, Sorrento

agricultural festas; in Calabria a variant is the Pecorara or Pasturara, a traditional shepherds' dance.

The amorous and passionate temperament of the Sicilian infuses a wealth of expression into his Tarantella, which is danced on any and every occasion. It is often accompanied by hand-clapping and danced by a limited number of couples who may improvise their own figures. The original of this famous dance is found in Sardinia, particularly in the Nuorese district, and it is here we come upon the traditional meaning of its name—cure from the bite of the tarantula. Accompanied by singing and beating of a tambourine, it is done by and for a bitten person who, by constant movement and rapid twirling, apparently can succeed in working off the poison of this dangerous spider.

⚜ *CHAIN DANCES* ⚜

This ancient form, embracing closed and open Rounds, comprises the **Ballu Sardu** or **Ballu Tondu**, also known as the **Duru-Duru**—an onomatopoeic word denoting the sound of the palm of the hand beating a tambourine—and the **Boroboboi**, from the syllable used as a kind of drone by the lowest voice of the accompanying singers. It may also be accompanied by the *launeddas*, and by the shepherd's *sulittu*, but the accordion is intruding here too. The Chain begins with an introduction in 2/4, the dance itself being in 6/8 time. The music consists of a series of short themes called *nodas*, which with a shorter coda are repeated many times and form *ritornelli*, or refrains. The musicians sit or stand in the middle and relieve one another, for the dance may go on for hours and hours, the chain for ever circling sunwise and counter-sunwise with slow and hieratic movement. The singers are oldish men forming a quartet or quintet who elaborate a theme set them.

At Cagliari on the Day of St. Efisio, the Patron of the city, a vast crowd blocks the principal piazza. Here a great

circle is formed which turns solemnly about the square, the
black and white of the men relieved by the brilliant scarlet
and flowery embroideries of their partners, whose white
head-veils make them dignified and enchanting figures.

DANCES OF RITUAL ORIGIN

Two of our Sword dances belong to the European Hilt-
and-Point family with its ritual elements, the Hoisting, the
Death and the making of the Lock or Rose. The 'Ndrezzata (Interweaving), traditional at Buonopane (Ischia), is
performed to a flute and drum with little bells and an odd
murmur—like the sound of a spinning wheel—hummed by
the dancers who hold a wooden sword in the left hand, a
small club in the right. They number 16 to 20; half the
company are called women and the chief dancer, the 'Cor-
poral', is hoisted on the Lock. There is no fixed date but
they used to perform on St. John Baptist's Day or Easter
Monday.

The Bal del Saber shows symbolic Sword dance elements
still more clearly. It belongs chiefly to Vicoforte, whence
it appears to have spread to Fenestrelle, Bagnasco, and
other villages in Piedmont. At Vicoforte, Harlequin (the
Fool) is tried, condemned, hoisted on the Lock, makes his
will and dies. They perform a Maypole figure and white-
clad Brighella, the old character from the *commedia dell'
arte*, still lives in this company with Moors, a Senator and
other personages up to twenty. A true dance-drama.

There are also fighting Sword dances, famous amongst
which is the Moresca of Lagosta, in the Adriatic,* where
the parties are not Moors and Christians but Moors and
Turks who fight for a lovely slave. In Corsica it shows
Moors versus Christians as in the great Morescas of Spain,

* The population is Croatian, but these Adriatic islands where
Morescas are found were for centuries in the possession of the seafaring
republics of Genoa and Venice.—*The Editor.*

and probably springs from an actual crusade against invading Moslems. To the same category belong the Morescas of Curzola (Korčula) and Genoa and the Parata of Malta with its little 'Bride'. The Moresca has an historical and literary aspect as well as a popular one, appearing at Court in the Middle Ages, and up to the sixteenth century in masques as a forerunner of the ballet.

We must note also the festival of the Madonna delle Milizie in Scicli, Sicily, in four 'pictures' representing a challenge and battle between Christians and Saracens.

The Spadonari of Piedmont show yet another type supposed to depict rebellion against a feudal tyrant, while the Lachera of Rocca Grimalda is a Carnival dance, without dialogue but with characters, two of which are Bride and Bridegroom, a noisy company of 'Muleteers' bringing up the rear and cracking their whips. The dancers, two 'Lacheri', must be agile and impervious to fatigue, as each time they approach the newly married couple they execute high leaps.

MUSIC

Our dances should be accompanied by regional instruments. Nowadays the accordion is heard everywhere and has largely superseded our old traditional instruments. Sometimes its asthmatical tones are supplemented by other instruments as for the Friulian Furlana. Sometimes Tarantella airs are played on mandolines and guitars with a drum—the sole instrument for a Saltarello.

Our most interesting and archaic instruments are the *sulittu* of Sardinian shepherds—a pipe with a wedge-shaped mouthpiece—and the polyphonic triple pipe called *launeddas*, giving forth its curious twittering sounds which seem to have engendered the steps of the Ballo Tondo. These two ancient instruments are becoming rarer and rarer, withdrawing to the southern part of the island, singers seated in the middle of the dancing circle taking their place.

In the Romagna we find one of the rare examples of a sung dance in the Mountain Trescone. This music is in two parts, a Stornella called 'cowherd's singing' and a melodic progression changing regularly from dominant to tonic, without words but using onomatopoeic syllables imitating the sounds of instruments. These syllables probably replace an instrumental refrain once used between the sung Stornelle and now fallen into disuse.*

We possess several sorts of bagpipes, very large in the Abruzzi and Calabria. The armed dances are usually accompanied by a drum and various instruments, but the Taratatà of Casteltermini is performed to and derives its name from the monotonous beat of a single drum.

COSTUME

The wonderful traditional costumes of Italy are in process of disappearing; banished from the cities, they can still be seen at country festivals. We were rich in costumes which varied from village to village, even in the same village where different social classes wore their own variants, so that the wearer's standing was at once recognised. Today they are chiefly worn for dancing, traditional costumes which have been handed down through generations coming out for special occasions. The women of Sorrento wear their ancestors' eighteenth-century dress when they dance the Tarantella, the corselet or laced bodice, the skirt (*vunnella*) of silk or satin, pleated and lined and covered in front by a lovely lace apron. The men are resplendent in tight satin breeches, usually green, long stockings, striped silk sash, white shirt, and on the head the well-known stocking cap hanging over one ear.

Sardinia, less exposed to outside influences, possesses a selection of costumes still worn in the country, the richest

* Cf. the set syllables used in the old Rigaudon tune sung for the Baccuber Sword dance in Dauphiné, France.—*The Editor*.

that of Cagliari and its district, especially the Quarto Sant' Elena. In Plate 4 a wide, red skirt will be noted, with a beautifully embroidered, deep white-silk border; an apron-front over the skirt, red, pleated and decorated with the same embroidery. A fine tulle embroidered veil covers head and shoulders, rich jewellery adds to the beautiful and imposing sight. In contrast the Sardinian man wears chiefly black and white. His gaiters are black, his wide breeches of white linen, a short skirt of black stuff goes over them; a linen shirt; his jersey-like waistcoat is of red or blue velvet; and over all goes his sleeveless thick, black jacket. On his head is the classic stocking cap, black instead of scarlet, often twenty-four inches long.

To the north, Friuli shows a costume already somewhat Alpine in character, modest and sober but with bright shoulder-shawl, flowers in the women's hair and on the men's hats.

The dress well known to foreigners and often believed to be Italy's 'national costume'—the white handkerchief thickly folded to lie flat on the head and to fall behind in the same thick fold, the laced bodice and very full skirt—in reality belonged to Rome and may still be seen occasionally in the Campagna.

The most original dancing costumes, as apart from traditional festival dresses, are seen in the various Sword dances. The 'Ndrezzata dancers of Ischia called women wear white knee-breeches, white stockings, leather sandals, a blue doublet adorned with a double row of small silver buttons, full white sleeves laced with blue at the wrists, and a rose-coloured sash. Those who dance as men wear a scarlet doublet, instead of blue, and a blue sash.

The Swordsmen of San Giorio are arresting in ceremonial white, with scarlet ribbons each ending in a little golden bell or some pendant which swings about with every movement. On their heads are hats of black felt gaily decorated with wild flowers.

SOME OCCASIONS WHEN DANCING MAY BE SEEN

January 21st, St. Vincent	The Swordsmen of San Vincenzo at Giaglione.
February 3rd, St. Biagio	The Swordsmen of Venaus in Val di Susa.
First Sunday in Lent	The Tresconeto danced in the whole Lunigiana region.
Good Friday	The Swordsmen of Limone, Piedmont.
April 23rd, St. George	The Swordsmen of San Giorio, Piedmont.
May 1st to 4th	Chain dances at Cagliari, Sardinia.
2nd Sunday in May	The Riattate at Villafranca Sicula, Sicily.

[For many years social-political leaders, rather than people with knowledge of local traditions, directed groups of workers and others in the practice of folk dance and song. A certain operatic influence also has been allowed to creep in at folk dance and music festivals. Great caution is needed at such exhibitions, and the folklorist in search of pure traditional material would be well advised to seek it in the villages of Italy.—*The Editor.*]

NOTE

Italian traditional costume ranges from Alpine to antique Mediterranean styles. Do not think then that the dress of Friuli will 'do' for a southern dance, nor vice versa. The swordsman of San Giorio wears his dancing costume. It is not that of other Italian men.

The Editor

THE DANCES

TECHNICAL EDITORS
MURIEL WEBSTER AND KATHLEEN P. TUCK

ABBREVIATIONS
USED IN DESCRIPTION OF STEPS AND DANCES

r—right⎱ referring to   R—right⎱ describing turns or
l—left ⎰ hand, foot, etc.   L—left ⎰ ground pattern
C—clockwise   C-C—counter-clockwise

For descriptions of foot positions and explanations of any ballet terms the following books are suggested for reference:

A Primer of Classical Ballet (Cecchetti method). Cyril Beaumont.

First Steps (R.A.D.). Ruth French and Felix Demery.

The Ballet Lover's Pocket Book. Kay Ambrose.

Reference books for description of figures:

The Scottish Country Dance Society's Publications. Many volumes, from Thornhill, Cairnmuir Road, Edinburgh 12.

The English Folk Dance and Song Society's Publications. Cecil Sharp House, 2 Regent's Park Road, London, N.W.1.

The Country Dance Book I–VI. Cecil J. Sharp. Novello & Co., London.

A variety of Arm Gestures is used in all Courting dances, especially by the women who alternately attract and repulse their partners, or play with their aprons, to give only a few examples.

In the Furlana, when partners dance together, the hands are held fairly high with a loose grasp to allow of much quick twisting and turning of both man and woman under the arms.

In the Tarantella, tambourines are often used. Further details of Arm Holds used in this dance are given with the Basic Steps with which they are associated.

All movements of body and arms are supple and graceful. In many of the steps the body sways from side to side, giving an appearance of flow and vitality.

BASIC STEPS

	Beats
Saltarello (used in Saltarello and Tarantella)	
Spring on r foot with l leg extended forward;	1
spring on l foot with r leg extended forward;	2
repeat on alternate feet.	
May be danced on the spot, travelling forward, backward and turning. The poise of body is well back.	

TURNING STEPS USED IN THE TARANTELLA

Pivot	
Turn on r foot to R, with l foot behind r foot taking the weight on the ball of l foot on the 'and' beat, and on the r foot on the 1st and 2nd beat.	1 & 2 &

Pirouette. This may be interpreted in many ways, the most usual resembling an Assemblé Turn:—Extend r foot quickly forward, knee straight; cross r foot over l foot and turn on balls of both feet.

During this turn the tambourine may be beaten above the head.

High Hops

Stamp on l foot, raising r knee forward and upward;

hop on l foot 3 times with r knee raised, turning to R about.

Repeat the step on r foot, turning L about.

The arms may be held above the head, elbows slightly bent, with tambourine in one hand. The shoulders are turned across the raised knee, i.e. to the R, when turning to R.

The number of hops on each foot may vary.

Long Hops

Hop on r foot, turning to R about, leaving the l leg extended backward off the ground. The body is tilted well forward. The hop may be repeated as often as desired.

Grasp. The man places his r arm round the back of his partner's waist, while she places her r arm round his waist. The tambourine is held well forward in the l hand. (This grasp belonged originally to the Neapolitan Tarantella.)

The step may be repeated on the l foot, partners grasping each other with the l arm and changing tambourines to the other hand.

Timing (right column):

(varied timing)

1

2 3 4

1 2 3 4

(ad lib.: 1 hop to each beat)

Heel-Toe Step

Hop on l foot, placing r foot forward on heel;	1
hop on l foot placing r toe to l toe.	2
Repeat, hopping on r foot.	1–2

Clap Kicks

a Spring feet together, beating the tambourine in front of face;	1
kick r leg forward and upward, beating tambourine under r knee.	2

Repeat the spring, kicking l leg forward and upward, beating tambourine under l knee.

This is an easier version than the following:

b Saltarello Steps, beating the tambourine under each leg as it is raised forward and upward.

BALLO TONDO

Region   District of Cagliari, Sardinia.

Character   Ceremonial dance for weddings, festivals and great occasions; stiff and solemn at first, growing gayer after many repeats.

Formation   A chain dance for men and women alternately, holding hands or linking fingers in a circular formation (see Plate 4).

Dance   The musicians, playing the *launeddas* and drum, stand in the middle of the room or square while a wide circle of dancers forms round them as described above. The whole circle moves

slowly C, two steps to the L and one step to R.
The women keep their eyes cast down, the men
look boldly ahead.

The Step

2 consecutive steps sideways to the L with springing
movements followed by one gliding step to the R. The
shoulders turn very slightly over the advancing foot. The
whole movement may develop into a gallop as the dancers
tire or as the music works up.

BALLO TONDO

Arranged by Arnold Foster

Play 4 times

FURLANA (*Ziguzaine*)

Region Friuli.

Character Courting dance: a lively mime is the essential part of the dance.

Formation For one or several couples.

Dance	MUSIC *Bars*
INTRODUCTION	
The man approaches with a little bunch of flowers which he presents to his partner, who pins it to her bodice.	Intro- duction (4 bars)
FIGURE I: PROMENADE	**A**
Man gives one hand to his partner and both skip C-C.	1–8
The woman then dances away from her partner with much coquetry; she allows herself to be caught on the last beat.	1–8
FIGURE II	**B**
Partners link little fingers of r hands and turn C with either Waltz or Skipping steps.	9–12
Repeat, linking l hands and turning C-C.	13–16
Linking r hands, man turns his partner under the raised arm.	9–10
Man turns under his own arm.	11–12
Linking l arms, man turns his partner under the raised arms.	13–14
Man turns under his own arm.	15–16

25

FURLANA

Arranged by Arnold Foster

26

C
p
16
(16)
17
18
19
p
20
21
22
23
24
D
25
26
27
28
29
30
E
31
32
33
34
poco a
35 poco accel. al fine
36
37
38
39
40

FIGURE III | C

Partners join both hands and skip C-C on the spot, facing one another. | 17–20

Repeat C. | 21–24

Link r arms and skip C. | 17–20

Link l arms and skip C-C. | 21–24

FIGURE IV: THE HANDKERCHIEF | D

The man produces a white handkerchief, knotted at two corners; each dancer holds one corner in the r hand and holds the handkerchief at head height.

Both skip C on the spot, the woman turning under the handkerchief on the last bar. | 25-28

Both skip C-C, holding handkerchief in l hands and woman turning under it on the last bar. | 29–32

The woman turns twice under the handkerchief while her partner turns once in the opposite direction. | 25

The woman then breaks away from her partner, twisting and turning as if to avoid being caught by the man, who follows her still holding the handkerchief (see Plate 3). | 26–32

FIGURE V: VALSE OF CONQUEST | E

The man seizes his partner by the waist and both waltz round the room, the tempo getting gradually faster and faster. | 33–40

Note.—The woman finishes every movement by turning under the man's arm, always in a forward direction. Most of the dance is done to a quick lively Skipping Step although the dancers may change to Waltz Step when they please.

Plate 3
Furlana, Friuli

Region	Sorrento.
Character	Courting dance, light, lively and dashing in movement. The mime of coquetry and love-making is an essential part of the dance. Some of the dancers carry tambourines.
Formation	A couple dance, first as two longwise sets, and later in two lines of couples facing one another (O = woman, □ = man):

Diagram 1

Diagram 2

Dance	MUSIC
FIGURE I: THE ENTRY	*Bars*
Two files of couples advancing as in Diagram 1 with 16 Saltarello steps, to finish facing partner a good distance apart.	1–8
The woman turns to L with a pirouette, beating tambourine;	9–10
the man turns to L with a pirouette, beating tambourine;	11–12
both pivot to R, shaking tambourines above heads;	13–15

TARANTELLA

Arranged by Arnold Foster

the man spins the woman to L under their | 16
joined r arms, finishing r shoulder to r
shoulder with partner.

FIGURE II: LONG HOPS

14 Long Hops on r foot, turning to R with | 17–23
r arm round partner's waist (see Basic Steps);
step and close feet together, separating from | 24
partner;
10 Long Hops on l foot, turning to L with l | 25–29
arm round partner's waist;
step and close feet together, separating from | 30
partner.
8 Saltarello steps, the woman dancing slight- | 31–34
ly backwards while the man dances the same
steps on the spot;
both pivot to R; | 35–36
both pivot to L. | 37–38

FIGURE III: GALLOP (start on 2nd beat of bar 38)

The woman moves sideways with Glissé or | 38–39
Gallop steps;
the man moves toward and behind her to | 40–41
place his r arm round her waist, holding his
tambourine high in the free hand;
both move away from one another with Glissé | 42–43
steps, man to L, woman to R, looking at one
another;
both dance toward one another and then | 44–51
away twice;
both dance away from one another. | 52–53

FIGURE IV: PROMENADE

The two files of couples cast outward to the | 54–61
back of the dance-space and then back to
original places with 16 Saltarello steps. Each

man holds his partner by the waist slightly in front of him.

All hold with feet together;	62
pirouette to R, beating tambourines;	63–64
pirouette to L, beating tambourines.	65–66

FIGURE V: VIS-À-VIS

a Each couple turns with partner and moves backward to face couple in the opposite file (see Diagram 2) with 8 Saltarello steps; — 67–70

the right-hand file now advances with 8 Saltarello steps, each dancer nodding to opposite partner; — 71–74

this line retires with 8 steps while the left-hand file advances; — 75–78

the left-hand file now retires with 8 steps. — 79–82

b Each woman kneels down on one knee while her partner dances round her with 16 Saltarello steps; — 83–90

the man now kneels, while the woman dances round with 8 steps; — 91–94

all pirouette or pivot on spot, beating tambourines. — 95–96

FIGURE VI: CLAP KICKS

Partners step and sway towards each other and away, hips just touching; repeat the movement. — 97–100

All dance Saltarello step, those with tambourines beating them under the knee as the leg is raised—four times in all; — 101–104

all beat tambourines at each side above waist level, still keeping the Saltarello step if possible. — 105

All pirouette to R, beating tambourines. — 106
(Those without tambourines clap own hands.)

SPADONARI DI SAN GIORIO (*Swordsmen of St. George*)

Region San Giorio, province of Turin, Piedmont.

Character A Sword dance (not of the 'hilt and point' variety) of a highly ceremonial type.

Formation Dance for six men.

Dance	MUSIC
The whole dance is performed to a drum-roll in march rhythm; there is no tune. The six dancers march in single file to the dance space, swords on r shoulders at a slope or upright in r hands.	
1 All turn in the air, alight and move into a square formation, shake their swords in front of their faces four times or more.	4 beats or more
2 With a high leap they alight inwards, making a smaller square. They join the points of their swords on the ground in the middle of the square; then join points at arm level.	4 beats
3 All leap back into larger square formation. Draw points of swords along the ground from R to L twice, as though tracing a furrow.	4 beats
4 All leap four times into the air, to alight facing East, West, South and North respectively.	4 beats
5 Facing inward they throw their swords up and across to their opposites, thus exchanging them.	4 beats
The whole dance may then be repeated, after which the six men march away in single file to the drum-roll.	

Plate 4   Ballo Tondo, Sardinia

BIBLIOGRAPHY

Borrelli, N.—'L'origine della Tarantella.' In *L'Italia Meridionale*, vol. VIII, 1929. (Origins of the Tarantella.)

Canziani, Estella.—*Through the Apennines and the Lands of the Abruzzi*. London, 1928.

—— *Piedmont*. London, 1913.

Galanti, B. M.—*La danza della spada in Italia*. Rome, 1942. (The Sword dance in Italy.)

—— 'Ancora sulla Moresca.' In *Lares*, vol. xv, 1949. (More about the Moresca.)

Liverani, F.—'La Tarantella, ballo·popolare napoletano.' In *Archivio delle tradizioni popolari*, vol. v, 1886. (The Tarantella, Neapolitan folk dance.)

Marzuttini, G. B.—*La vera Furlana nelle sue due forme originali*. Trieste, 1914. (The real Furlana in its two original forms.)

Nataletti, G.—'Il Saltarello romanesco.' In *Momento Musicale*, November 1929. (The Roman Saltarello.)

—— 'Il Saltarello a Roma e nella Campagna Romana.' In *Strenna dei Romanisti*, 1942. (The Saltarello in Rome and in the Roman Campagna.)

Pitrè, G.—*Spettacoli e feste popolari siciliane*. Palermo, 1881. (Folk festivals and spectacles in Sicily.)

Pratella Balilla, F.—*Saggio di gridi, canzoni, cori e danze del popolo italiano*. Bologna, 1920. (Street cries, songs, chorus and dance in Italy.)

Ungarelli, G.—*Le vecchie danze italiane ancora in uso nella provincia Bolognese*. Rome, 1894. (Old Italian dances still in use in the province of Bologna.)

Vidossi, G.—'La danza degli spadonari a Venaus in Val di Susa.' In *Lares*, vol. VII, 1936. (Dance of the Swordsmen at Venaus, Val di Susa.)